THE
APACHE

BY JOHN O'MARA

Enslow
PUBLISHING

Please visit our website, www.enslow.com. For a free color catalog of all our high-quality books, call toll free 1-800-398-2504 or fax 1-877-980-4454.

Library of Congress Cataloging-in-Publication Data
Names: O'Mara, John, author.
Title: The Apache / John O'Mara.
Description: New York : Enslow Publishing, [2022] | Series: Native american
    peoples | Includes bibliographical references and index.
Identifiers: LCCN 2020028561 (print) | LCCN 2020028562 (ebook) | ISBN
    9781978521766 (library binding) | ISBN 9781978521742 (paperback) | ISBN
    9781978521759 (set) | ISBN 9781978521773 (ebook)
Subjects: LCSH: Apache Indians–Juvenile literature. | CYAC: Apache
    Indians. | Indians of North America–New Mexico.
Classification: LCC E99.A6 O63 2022 (print) | LCC E99.A6 (ebook) | DDC
    979.0049725–dc23
LC record available at https://lccn.loc.gov/2020028561
LC ebook record available at https://lccn.loc.gov/2020028562

Published in 2022 by
Enslow Publishing
29 E. 21st Street
New York, NY 10010

Designer: Katelyn E. Reynolds
Interior Layout: Tanya Dellaccio
Editor: Therese Shea

Photo credits: Cover, p. 1 (texture) aopsan/Shutterstock.com; cvr, pp. 1–24 (striped texture) Eky Studio/Shutterstock.com; p. 5 (top) https://upload.wikimedia.org/wikipedia/commons/f/ff/Apachean_ca.18-century.png; p. 5 (bottom) MPI/Archive Photos/Getty Images; p. 6 Historical/Corbis Historical/Getty Images; p. 7 Oklahoma Historical Society/Archive Photos/Getty Images; p. 8 Zen Rial/Moment/Getty Images; p. 9 Buyenlarge/Archive Photos/Getty Images; p. 11 https://upload.wikimedia.org/wikipedia/commons/3/39/Group_of_Miguel%27s_Band_Coyotero_Apaches_near_Camp_Apache_Arizona_1873_-_NARA_-_519786.jpg; pp. 13, 15 Transcendental Graphics/Archive Photos/Getty Images; p. 14 Hulton Archive/Getty Images; p. 17 GraphicaArtis/Archive Photos/Getty Images; p. 18 Bettmann/Getty Images; p. 19 DenisTangneyJr/E+/Getty Images; p. 21 (top) Universal History Archive/Universal Images Group/Getty Images; p. 21 (bottom) Culture Club/Hulton Archive/Getty Images; p. 23 MPI/Archive Photos/Getty Images; p. 24 Travis Coan/Shutterstock.com; p. 27 Robert Alexander/Archive Photos/Getty Images; p. 28 BRENDAN SMIALOWSKI/AFP/Getty Images; p. 29 VisionsofAmerica/Joe Sohm/Photodisc/Getty Images.

Portions of this work were originally authored by Mark J. Harasymiw and published as *The Apache People*. All new material in this edition authored by John O'Mara.

Printed in the United States of America

CPSIA compliance information: Batch #CSENS22: For further information contact Enslow Publishing, New York, New York, at 1-800-398-2504.

Find us on

CONTENTS

WORDS IN THE GLOSSARY APPEAR IN **BOLD** TYPE THE FIRST TIME THEY ARE USED IN THE TEXT.

WHAT'S IN A NAME?

The Apache aren't just one group of Native Americans. This name is used for several groups of **related** Native Americans. And it isn't even a name they gave themselves. "Apache" likely comes from a word spoken by the Zuni people: *ápachu*. This means "enemy." However, it was the Spanish who used it for the Apache.

When Spanish explorers first came upon Apache in the 1500s, the Apache were living across areas that are now the southwestern United States and northern Mexico. These lands were claimed by Spain and made part of Mexico.

GET THE FACTS!

Apache **ancestors** lived in western Canada and moved south about 1100 CE. We know this because the Apache language is closely related to a language spoken by people native to western Canada. Sometime after 1100 CE, the Apache separated into two main groups.

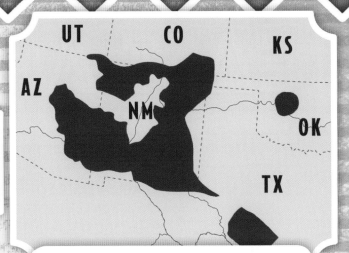

THIS MAP SHOWS IN GREEN WHERE APACHE GROUPS LIVED IN THE 1700s.

SPANISH EXPLORERS, 1541

EAST AND WEST

The two main groups of Apache are sometimes called eastern and western Apache. They spoke different languages. The eastern Apache lived on the southern Great Plains and hunted bison. They traded meat and skins for the corn and pottery of the Pueblo peoples. The eastern Apache **traditional** way of life changed, however.

A 19TH-CENTURY KIOWA-APACHE CHIEF NAMED PACER (OR PESO) IS SHOWN IN THIS PHOTO.

GET THE FACTS!

The Kiowa called themselves *Kai-i-gwu*, which means "principal people." They learned the ways of the Plains peoples, including the Comanche, and made peace with them. They hunted bison and other animals and lived in **tepees**. Like other Plains peoples, they moved often.

KIOWA CAMP NEAR FORT SILL IN OKLAHOMA

In the 1700s, the Comanche drove the Apache from the Great Plains. Most moved west into today's eastern New Mexico, Texas, and northern Mexico. Some moved east, where they became **allies** of the Kiowa. These Apache became the Kiowa-Apache.

The western Apache moved around less than the eastern Apache. They lived in rocky deserts of Arizona and western New Mexico. They became skilled at finding plants to eat there. They even used certain plants, such as cactus, as water sources.

One important Apache food was mescal from the agave plant. The Apache dug up the plant's white bulb. It could be as large as 3 feet (0.9 m) around! The mescal was dried and eaten or made into a sweet liquid. The Apache cooked about 1 ton (907 kg) of mescal at a time in a big pit.

AGAVE PLANT

GET THE FACTS!

Western Apache lived in homes called wickiups. To make them, they made a frame of bent trees that looked like an upside-down U. They covered the trees with grasses, plants, or animal skins. These homes could be moved from place to place.

THIS IS AN EXAMPLE OF AN APACHE WICKIUP.

BANDS AND FAMILIES

For the most part, the Apache people lived in groups called bands. A band was made up of family members. Each band chose a man as its leader. A leader could lose his position by making bad decisions. Sometimes several bands were united under one chief.

GET THE FACTS!

Apache bands came together for certain events. They sometimes united to fight against a common enemy. They came together for **religious** reasons too. Some Apache bands didn't speak the same language or have the same beliefs, however.

FAMOUS APACHE BANDS

- SAN CARLOS
- TONTO
- CIBECUE
- JANERO
- WHITE MOUNTAIN
- BIDANKU
- NATAGE
- NORTEÑO
- COYOTERO

THIS PHOTO OF PART OF A COYOTERO APACHE BAND WAS TAKEN IN 1878.

The Apache people are matrilineal. That means their family lines are traced through the mother's side. When an Apache man got married, he lived with his wife's family. Their children belonged to the wife's family. Grandparents were often the teachers of the young.

APACHE BELIEFS

Different bands of Apache had different religious beliefs. However, most honored a Creator spirit. They asked the Creator for help and powers. Many Apache never talked about death or called dead people by name. When a parent died, the children's names were changed so their names wouldn't remind them of their dead parent.

The Apache believed illness could be spread by seeing a dead body or by touching a dead person's things. So, when an Apache died, the body was buried quickly. Everything the person had owned was buried or removed.

Mescalero Apache believe certain animals are bad **omens**. Owls and snakes are two such creatures. They're thought to bring bad luck and should be avoided. Other animals, such as bears, are left alone because they're highly respected.

FEATHER HEADDRESS

APACHE PERFORM A **CEREMONY** WITH A BISON. MOST APACHE DIDN'T WEAR FEATHER HEADDRESSES. THE CHIRICAHUA ADOPTED THE PRACTICE FROM THE KIOWA PEOPLE.

TRYING TO SURVIVE

For a long time, the Apache hunted the large hairy animals called bison. They used almost every part of a bison's body for food, clothing, and other needed objects. When the Apache were driven away from the Plains, they had to look for food in other places.

USES FOR BISON

- FOOD
- BONES FOR TOOLS
- HIDE FOR BLANKETS AND CLOTHES
- BISON HAIR FOR ROPE

APACHE HUNTERS USED LONG SPEARS AS WELL AS BOWS AND ARROWS WHEN HUNTING BISON.

Many hungry Apache communities became skilled at **raiding** Spanish ranches. A group of four to twelve men traveled many miles on foot. They'd steal cattle and horses and race back to their homes. They often split up so they were harder to track.

GERONIMO TAKES A STAND

In 1848, the Mexican-American War came to an end. Mexico sold much of the land the Apache lived on to the United States. Soon after, Americans began settling in Apache territory.

The Apache were forced to live on certain lands set aside for them, called reservations. Some fought to keep their traditional lands. Others fought because reservation conditions were poor. The last warring group of Apache, led by Geronimo, gave up fighting in 1886. Geronimo and his band were sent to work in Florida.

GERONIMO WAS A CHIRICAHUA APACHE LEADER WHO REFUSED TO LIVE ON A RESERVATION FOR MORE THAN 10 YEARS. HE FOUGHT FOR THE APACHE TRADITIONAL WAY OF LIFE.

GERONIMO

BORN: JUNE 1829
NO-DOYOHN CANYON, MEXICO

DIED: FEBRUARY 17, 1909
FORT SILL, OKLAHOMA

GET THE FACTS!

Geronimo's Apache name was Goyathlay, which means "one who yawns." Mexican soldiers killed his mother, wife, and children. Geronimo wrote a book near the end of his life. It's called *Geronimo: His Own Story*. He died in 1909.

COCHISE FIGHTS BACK

Like Geronimo, Cochise was a famous leader of a Chiricahua band of the Apache. When Americans began to settle in the Southwest, Cochise tried to keep peace between his people and the white settlers.

GET THE FACTS!

In 1861, Cochise was falsely blamed for stealing cattle. He was put in prison but escaped. He spent years fighting the army and white settlers on Apache lands. Finally, he settled on a reservation for the Chiricahua Apache in Arizona.

COCHISE AND HIS FOLLOWERS HID FROM THE U.S. ARMY IN THE DRAGOON MOUNTAINS OF ARIZONA.

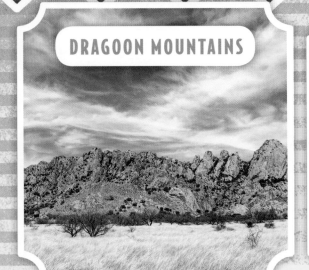

DRAGOON MOUNTAINS

COCHISE

BORN: AROUND 1810
SOUTHEASTERN ARIZONA
OR NORTHWESTERN MEXICO

DIED: JUNE 8, 1874
DRAGOON MOUNTAINS, ARIZONA

However, an American army officer arrested Cochise in 1861, even though the two were meeting after a **truce**. Cochise escaped—with three bullets in his body. He fought the Americans for the next 10 years. In 1872, he finally signed an agreement with the U.S. government. He lived peacefully until his death 2 years later.

APACHE RESERVATIONS

It wasn't easy for the Apache to make their reservations feel like home. The U.S. government tried to make them give up their traditions. Many Apache children were forced to go to schools far away. Apache weren't allowed to speak their languages or wear traditional clothing.

Few people on reservations had jobs. Most were poor. Bad conditions led to the spread of illness. In 1920, nearly 90 percent of Jicarilla (hee-keh-REE-yeh) Apache children had tuberculosis, an illness of the lungs. The populations on all Apache reservations fell.

CHIRICAHUA APACHE ON RESERVATION

THIS PHOTO OF A JICARILLA APACHE IS FROM THE EARLY 1900s. THESE APACHE WERE PLACED ON A RESERVATION IN NORTHERN NEW MEXICO.

GET THE FACTS!

Before reservations, most Apache were nomadic. This means they traveled from place to place to find food. They couldn't practice this way of life on reservations. However, after years of fighting the U.S. Army, they had no choice.

NEW LAWS

    In 1887, a law called the Dawes Act divided reservations into plots of farmland for Native Americans. In 1934, Congress passed the Indian Reorganization Act. This law allowed the Apache and other native tribes to form their own governments.

    In 1978, the American Indian Religious Freedom Act allowed Native Americans to go to their sacred, or holy, places to practice their religion. Other laws have made it easier for Native Americans to operate businesses. Apache groups have used these laws to try to improve the lives of their people.

A TIMELINE OF THE APACHE PEOPLE

AROUND 1100 → APACHE MOVE SOUTH FROM TODAY'S CANADA.

1500s ← SPANISH EXPLORERS MEET APACHE IN TODAY'S AMERICAN SOUTHWEST.

1700s → COMANCHE PUSH APACHE OUT OF BISON TERRITORY.

1848 ← THE UNITED STATES WINS TERRITORY IN THE SOUTHWEST AFTER A WAR WITH MEXICO.

1870s → THE APACHE ARE FORCED ONTO RESERVATIONS.

1872 ← COCHISE SIGNS A PEACE AGREEMENT WITH THE UNITED STATES.

1886 → GERONIMO AND THE LAST OF THE WARRING APACHE GIVE UP TO THE U.S. ARMY.

1887 ← THE DAWES ACT DIVIDES RESERVATIONS INTO PLOTS OF FARMLAND FOR NATIVE AMERICANS.

1934 → THE INDIAN REORGANIZATION ACT IS PASSED.

1978 ← THE AMERICAN INDIAN RELIGIOUS FREEDOM ACT IS PASSED.

THE DAWES ACT OF 1887 ALSO GAVE NATIVE AMERICAN LAND TO WHITE SETTLERS AND TO RAILROAD COMPANIES.

GET THE FACTS!

Under the Dawes Act, many Native Americans were stuck with land that wasn't good for farming. The government thought making Native Americans into farmers would force them to give up their traditions. Not accepting land meant they couldn't be U.S. citizens.

23

WESTERN APACHE RESERVATIONS

Most Apache who live on reservations today are found in Arizona and New Mexico. There are three reservations in Arizona: the San Carlos Apache Reservation, the Tonto Apache Reservation, and the White Mountain Apache Reservation.

THE APACHE INVITE PEOPLE TO THE SAN CARLOS RESERVATION TO ENJOY THE LAKE CREATED BY THE COOLIDGE DAM.

COOLIDGE DAM

GET THE FACTS!

The Tonto Apache Reservation is the smallest reservation in Arizona. About 100 Apache live there. The reservation is located near where Tonto Apache ancestors lived for hundreds of years. Today, the Tonto Apache are known for their beautiful art.

NEW MEXICO APACHE RESERVATIONS

- MESCALERO APACHE TRIBE
- JICARILLA APACHE NATION

ARIZONA APACHE RESERVATIONS

- SAN CARLOS APACHE RESERVATION
- TONTO APACHE RESERVATION
- WHITE MOUNTAIN APACHE RESERVATION

The Coolidge Dam, built on the San Carlos reservation, created a large lake. The Apache sell permits to people who want to fish, hunt, hike, and camp there. The San Carlos Apache Cultural Center teaches visitors about Apache religion and traditions. The center also features and sells the work of Apache craftspeople.

The White Mountain Apache Reservation is found in eastern Arizona. It's home mainly to western Apache who have lived there for thousands of years. Farming and raising cattle are important businesses there. Apache on this land also run a winter and summer **resort**. The mountains, lakes, and streams draw people who want to ski, fish, and boat. There's also a large **casino** that attracts many visitors.

The White Mountain Apache Cultural Center displays historic objects and modern Apache arts and crafts. A re-creation of an Apache village is located nearby.

THE PEOPLE OF THE WHITE MOUNTAIN APACHE RESERVATION KEEP THEIR WAYS OF LIFE ALIVE THROUGH TRADITIONAL SONGS, DANCES, CEREMONIES, AND LANGUAGE.

WHITE MOUNTAIN APACHE RESERVATION NUMBERS

- 16,000 PEOPLE
- 2,600 SQUARE MILES (6,734 SQ KM)
- 26 LAKES
- 400 MILES (644 KM) OF WATERWAYS

GET THE FACTS!

The southwest part of the White Mountain Apache Reservation is about 2,600 feet (792 m) above sea level. Its highest point is Mount Baldy on the eastern border, which is sacred to the Apache people. It's about 11,400 feet (3,475 m) high.

EASTERN APACHE RESERVATIONS

The two Apache reservations in New Mexico are home to the Mescalero Apache Tribe and the Jicarilla Apache Nation. The Mescalero Apache Reservation is located in southern New Mexico. The Jicarilla Apache Nation Reservation is located in northern New Mexico. Both reservations have successful businesses, including a ski resort, timber businesses, and oil wells.

TODAY, APACHE PEOPLE ARE STILL FIGHTING FOR LANDS THAT ARE SACRED TO THEIR PEOPLE, SUCH AS OAK FLAT IN ARIZONA.

GET THE FACTS!

You can learn more about the Apache by visiting their reservations on certain days. Events on the Jicarilla reservation include the Little Beaver Roundup, which features dances and a **rodeo**. On the Mescalero reservation, people attend the Apache Ceremonial Dances and Rodeo.

About 30,000 Apache live in the United States today, on and off reservations. Their ancestors fought hard to keep their culture alive. We can honor them by respecting their traditions and learning more about them.

GLOSSARY

ally Any of two or more people or groups who work together.

ancestor A relative who lived long before someone.

casino A place where people gamble, or play games of chance and risk.

ceremony An event to honor or celebrate something.

omen Something believed to be a sign of something that will happen in the future.

raid To suddenly attack.

related Connected by being in the same family.

religious Having to do with a belief in and way of honoring a god or gods.

resort A place where people can stay for entertainment, exercise, and fun activities.

rodeo A contest of many events involving cowboy skills.

tepee A tent shaped like a cone that was used in the past by some Native Americans as a home.

traditional Having to do with long-practiced customs.

truce An agreement to end fighting for a period of time.

FOR MORE INFORMATION

BOOKS

Bial, Raymond. *The People and Culture of the Apache*. New York, NY: Cavendish Square, 2016.

Bodden, Valerie. *Apache*. Mankato, MN: Creative Education/ Creative Paperbacks, 2018.

Richmond, Wren. *Apache*. New York, NY: PowerKids Press, 2016.

WEBSITES

Apache Peoples
www.ducksters.com/history/native_american_apache.php
Find out more about the Apache way of life.

Mescalero Apache Tribe—Our Culture
mescaleroapachetribe.com/our-culture/
Learn more about the Mescalero Apache.

Native American Facts for Kids
www.bigorrin.org/apache_kids.htm
Read these questions and answers about the Apache people.

INDEX